Developing Nun

NUMBERS AND THE NUMBER SYSTEM

ACTIVITIES FOR THE DAILY MATHS LESSON

year

1

Paul Broadbent

A & C BLACK

D0189223

Contents

Estimating

Resource sheets

Reprinted 2000, 2001
Published 1999 by A&C Black (Publishers) Limited
37 Soho Square, London W1D 3QZ

ISBN O-7136-5232-2

Copyright text © Paul Broadbent, 1999
Copyright illustrations © Martin Pierce, 1999
Copyright cover illustration © Charlotte Hard, 1999

The authors and publisher would like to thank the following teachers for their advice in producing this series of books:
Tracy Adam; Shilpa Bharambe; Hardip Channa; Sue Hall; Ann Hart; Lydia Hunt; Madeleine Madden; Helen Mason;
Anne Norbury; Jane Siddons; Judith Wells; Fleur Whatley.

A CIP catalogue record for this book is available from the British Library.

All rights reserved. This book may be photocopied, for use in the school or educational establishment for which it was purchased,
but may not be reproduced in any other form or by any means – graphic, electronic or mechanical, including recording, taping
or information retrieval systems – without the prior permission in writing of the publishers.

Printed in Great Britain by St Edmundsbury Press Ltd, Bury St Edmunds, Suffolk.

Introduction

Developing Numeracy: Numbers and the Number System is a series of seven photocopiable activity books designed to be used during the daily maths lesson. They focus on the first strand of the National Numeracy Strategy *Framework for teaching mathematics*. The activities are intended to be used in the time allocated to pupil activities; they aim to reinforce the teaching within the lesson and provide practice and consolidation of the objectives contained in the framework document.

Year 1 supports the teaching of mathematics to children in this age group by providing a series of activities to develop essential skills in counting and recognising numbers. On the whole they are designed for children to work independently, although due to the age of the children this is obviously not always possible, and some teacher support may be needed.

Year 1:

- develops the sense of the size of a number and the counting system including place value and estimating;
- explores properties of numbers and number sequences;
- includes activities which focus on the reading, writing, comparing and ordering of numbers;
- promotes independent work during the daily maths lesson with low guidance activities;
- encourages the use of the correct mathematical language.

Extension

Many of the activity sheets end with a challenge (**Now try this!**) which reinforces and extends the children's learning, and provides the teacher with the opportunity for assessment. Where children are asked to carry out an activity the instructions are clear to enable them to work independently, although it may be helpful for this age group if the teacher reads out the instructions and explains the activity to the children before they begin working on it.

Organisation

For many of the activities it will be useful to have available coloured pencils, interlocking cubes, dice, counters, scissors and glue. Several of the sheets involve cutting out and sticking, which can be done by the children or adults as appropriate. Several activities can be re-used if the appropriate areas of the pages are masked before copying and different numbers substituted to provide variety or differentiation. It may often be helpful to provide the children with number lines to help them to complete the activities. Photocopiable resource sheets (including a certificate to recognise individual children's achievements) are provided at the end of the book.

To help teachers to select appropriate learning experiences for their children the activities are grouped into sections within each book. The pages are not intended to be presented in the order in which they appear unless otherwise stated.

Teachers' notes

Very brief notes are provided at the bottom of most pages, giving ideas and suggestions for maximising the effectiveness of the activity sheets. These notes could be masked before photocopying.

Structure of the daily maths lesson

The recommended structure of the daily maths lesson for Key Stage 1 is as follows:

Start to lesson, oral work, mental calculation	5-10 minutes
Main teaching and pupil activities	about 30 minutes
Plenary	about 10 minutes

The activities in the **Developing Numeracy** books are designed to be carried out during the time allocated to pupil activities.

The following chart shows an example of the way in which an activity from this book can be used to achieve the required organisation of the daily maths lesson for Year 1 children.

In the garden (page 36)

Start to the lesson	
As a whole class introduction to the lesson, use a blank number line or counting stick with ten divisions. Name one end zero and the other end ten and ask the children to count aloud as you point to the divisions, both forwards and backwards. Challenge the children to call out the numbers as you point to random positions on the line. Develop the activity by naming one end ten and the other end twenty and counting through the teen numbers.	**5-10 minutes**

Main teaching and pupil activities	
Give each pupil a 10 arrow card and a set of unit arrow cards (page 62). Ask them to make the number 15. Show them that this is the same as 10 add 5, then repeat for other numbers. Extend the activity by using the language of comparison: "*Show me... a number less than 14... a number greater than 16... a number between 17 and 19*". The children could work in small groups, each child making a different number between 10 and 20. Ask who has the highest and the lowest numbers in the group. The children arrange themselves so that they are standing with the numbers they have made in order. The children then work on **In the garden** (page 36, **Developing Numeracy: Numbers and the Number System Year 1**).	**about 30 minutes**

Plenary	
During the plenary session, the children explain the work they did for the activity **In the garden**, then talk about teen numbers: "*13 is 10 and 3, it is one less than 14, it is one more than 12, it is greater than 11*".	**about 10 minutes**

Further activities

The following activities provide some practical ideas for teaching children how to count and recognise numbers. They are intended to introduce or reinforce the main teaching part of the lesson.

Counting, properties of numbers and number sequences

Action rhymes
There are many action rhymes that can help to build children's confidence and pleasure in counting as they sing, chant or join in with the actions. These include 'Ten green bottles', 'One, two, three, four, five, Once I caught a fish alive', 'The beehive', 'Five fat sausages', 'One, two, buckle my shoe' and 'On the first day of Christmas'.

Count in turn
Children stand in a line facing the same direction; they stamp gently as they count and throw their arms up in the air for the last number in the counting sequence. As the last number is said, they turn and begin the counting sequence again, keeping to a regular rhythm. They could also clap in time to the count.

Boston wave
Children sit in a circle and count slowly in unison, "*one, two, three, four, five; one, two, three, four, five,*" and so on. Decide in which direction the Boston wave will go; as *one* is chanted, point to a child who quickly stands up and sits down. Point to the next child as *two* is chanted, who again has quickly to stand up and sit down. Continue around the circle. With practice, there will be no need to point; children will automatically continue the Boston wave around the circle.

Thigh, clap, snap, snap
Sit in a circle and slowly slap the tops of your legs, then clap hands and snap fingers, first with one hand and then with the other, developing a steady rhythm. Count each number from one to four in time to the actions:

thigh	clap	snap	snap	thigh	clap	snap	snap
1	2	3	4	1	2	3	4

These counting activities can be developed to give practice in counting backwards and forwards (see pages 16 and 17), counting in fives and tens (pages 15 and 23), counting in threes (page 24) and counting in twos (pages 18-20).

Place value and ordering

Behind the wall
Slide a number card up from behind a 'wall' (which could be any suitable screen such as a piece of card or a book). Slide the number up slowly so that it just peeps over the top of the 'wall' and ask which number it might be. Keep showing a little more of the number until the children work out which number it is. Repeat for other numbers.

Show me
Give each child a set of numeral cards 0 to 10, (page 63). Play 'show me' activities where each child shows a numeral card by holding it up in the air as you say, "*Show me the number 8*", "*show me the number 3*", "*show me 0*", etc. Hold up a numeral card yourself and ask the children to show a number like it; what does it say? The children could hold up numeral cards to show the answers to questions such as: "*Show me a number... greater than 3... smaller than 8... between 6 and 9*". "*Show me one more than 7... one less than 4*".

Numbers all around us
Talk to the children about where they can see numbers in the environment, around the home and in the street as well as in parks, public buildings, shops and restaurants (for example, they could look for numbers on front doors, telephones, road signs, petrol pumps, cars, televisions, microwaves, clocks, price tags and menus).

All about the number
The children could make a scrapbook or poster of numerals cut from magazines, catalogues and birthday cards, with each number having a page of its own. They could draw pictures to illustrate the numbers.

Numbers in the air
On large pieces of paper, use one colour to write a number such as 1, that is written in a continuous stroke, and two colours to write the numbers that need two strokes, such as 4 and 5 (writing the first stroke in one colour and the second in another). Ask individual children to stand and point to each number, tracing the separate strokes in the air. This will help the children to see the different strokes needed when writing numerals. Discuss the variations in number formation between left- and right-handed children.

Arrow cards
Give each child a set of arrow cards (page 62). Ask the children to make different numbers, showing the value of the tens and units. Extend by using the language of comparison: "*Show me... a number less than 40... a number greater than 70... a number between 50 and 60*". The children could work in small groups, each child making a different TU number. Questions could be asked, such as, "*Who has got the highest and the lowest numbers in each group?*" Ask the children in each group to stand in order of the numbers they have made.

People numbers
Give out one set of large numeral cards 0 to 10. The children holding the numeral cards stand facing the rest of the class. Ask them to arrange themselves in order, from 0 to 10. Ask individual children who are not holding a number to change places with a numeral chosen by you. ("*Sam change places with the number three; Emma change places with the number eight.*") Use the language of position, such as before and after, within this. ("*Ali change places with any number before the number three.*")

Washing lines
String up a washing line in part of the classroom and give the children numbers to hang on the washing line using small bulldog clips. Ask the children to hang the numbers in order. When all the numbers are in position, ask the children to identify particular numbers. ("*Point to the number 14; point to the number between 12 and 14; point to the number before 19.*") In all these activities, use the language of comparison (such as more or less, greater or smaller) and the language of order (first, last, before, after, next, between).

Queues
Arrange the children in a queue and ask who is first, second, third... last. Tell the children to turn round so that they are facing the opposite direction and ask them again who is first, second and so on.

Estimating

Handfuls
Ask a child to take a handful of beads or counters. The rest of the class try to estimate how many have been taken. The total can be checked by counting.

Estimates and measures
Set the children challenges, asking them to estimate and then measure, for example, how far they can jump or throw a beanbag, how many cubes would fit across the table top and how many cups of water would fill a jug.

How many toys?

- **Write how many.** [7] balls

[ ] teddies [ ] tractors [ ] ducks [ ] dolls

balls

teddies

tractors

ducks

dolls

- **Colour 2 toys yellow.**
- **Colour 6 toys brown.**
- **Colour 3 toys blue.**
- **Colour 10 toys red.**

Teachers' note Provide a selection of different types of toys (for example, cuddly toys, toys with wheels) and ask the children to count each group. Vary the activity by introducing different ways of grouping toys; for example, by colour, size or shape. Some children might need a number line to help them complete the activity.

Developing Numeracy
Numbers and the Number System
Year 1
© A & C Black 1999

7

Towers of bricks

- Write the numbers on the bricks.
- Write how many in each tower.
- Join each set of bricks to the correct number.

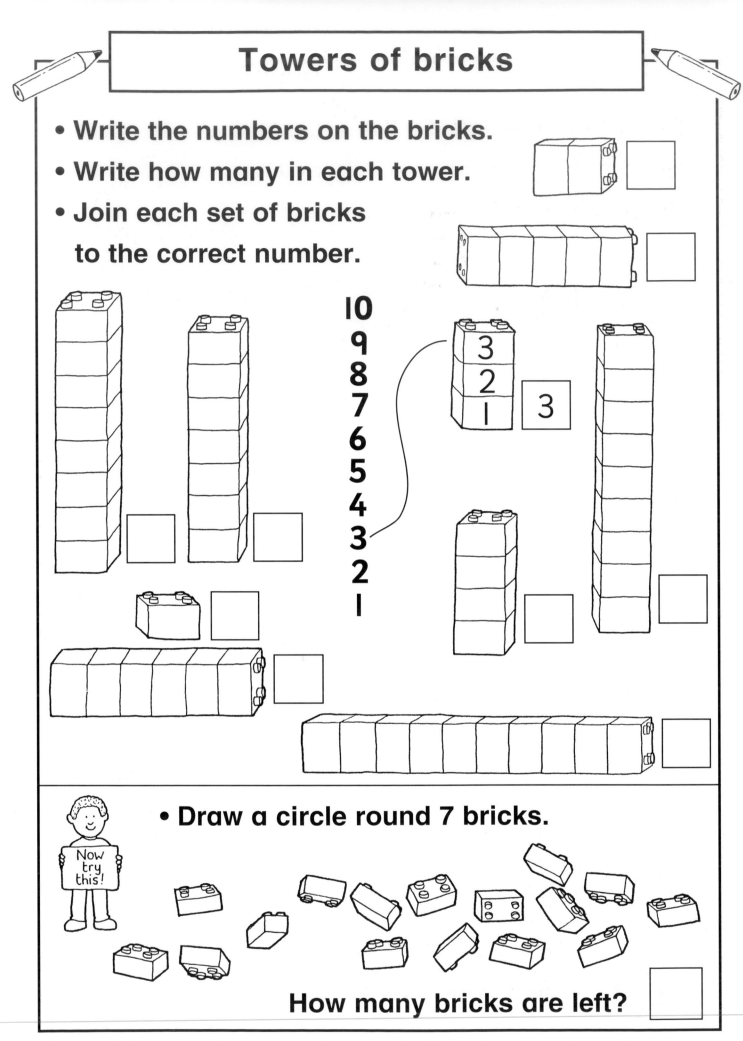

10
9
8
7
6
5
4
3
2
1

- Draw a circle round 7 bricks.

Now try this!

How many bricks are left?

Teachers' note Use bricks or interlocking cubes to model the pictures if children need further support in completing this activity.

Developing Numeracy
Numbers and the Number System
Year 1
© A & C Black 1999

8

Lift off!

- **Read the numbers on the rockets.**
- **Start at** 10 **and read backwards.**
- **Write the missing numbers.**

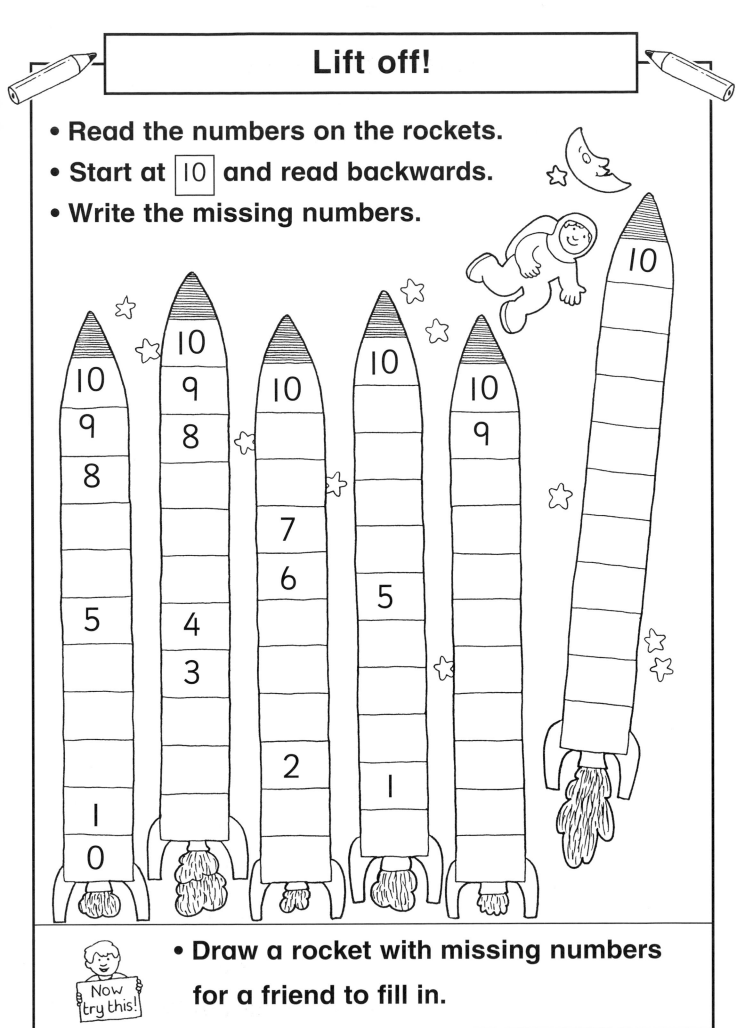

- **Draw a rocket with missing numbers for a friend to fill in.**

Now try this!

Teachers' note As an introduction to the activity, sing 'Ten green bottles' with a group or the whole class. The children could draw their own set of bottles and cross out each bottle as it falls, starting at ten.

Developing Numeracy
Numbers and the Number System
Year 1
© A & C Black 1999

Number line fishing

- **Count along the number line. Start from 0.**
- **Join the fish to the correct place on the number line.**

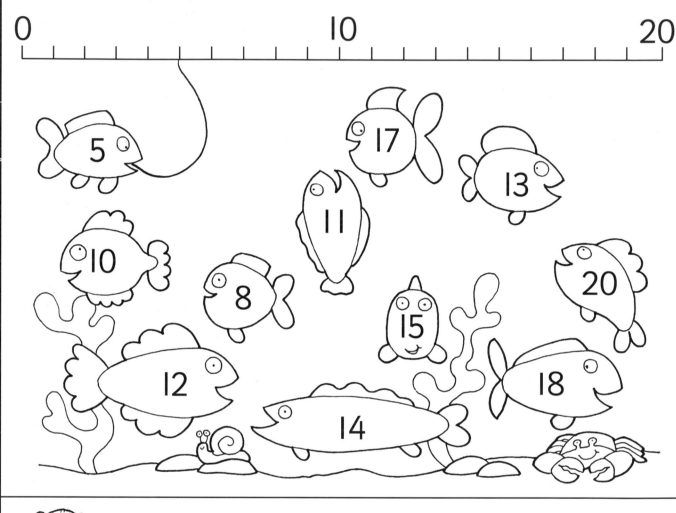

- **Count along the number line.**
- **Write the correct numbers in the boxes.**

Teachers' note To introduce the activity, count orally along the number line as a group, encouraging the children to point to each position as the number is said. Challenge the children to count on or back from a given position.

Developing Numeracy
Numbers and the Number System
Year 1
© A & C Black 1999

Space race game

- **Take turns to roll a dice and move your counter.**
- **If you land on a star and count correctly, move on 2 places.**

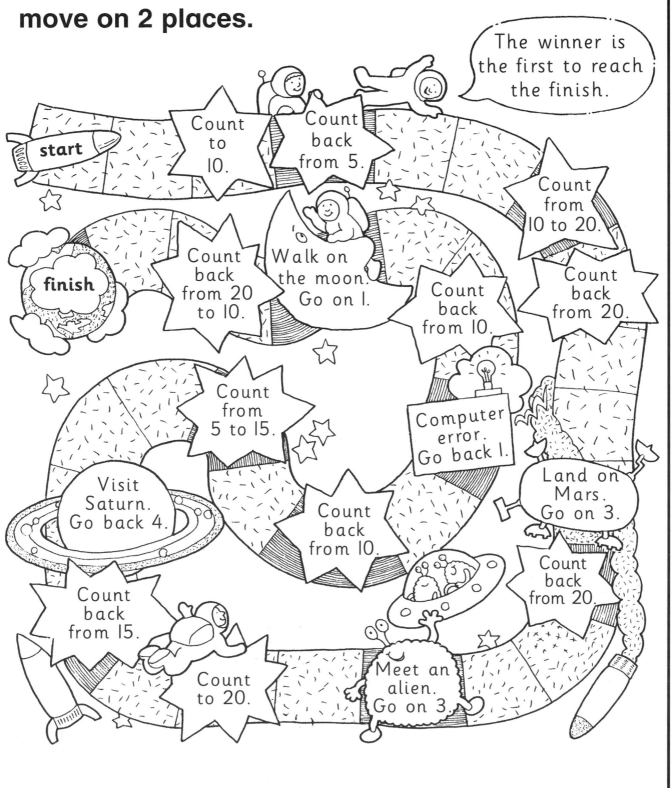

The winner is the first to reach the finish.

start

Count to 10.

Count back from 5.

Count from 10 to 20.

finish

Count back from 20 to 10.

Walk on the moon. Go on 1.

Count back from 10.

Count back from 20.

Count from 5 to 15.

Computer error. Go back 1.

Land on Mars. Go on 3.

Visit Saturn. Go back 4.

Count back from 10.

Count back from 20.

Count back from 15.

Count to 20.

Meet an alien. Go on 3.

Teachers' note This is a game for two or more players. Each group will need a counter for each player and a number line or track from 0 to 20. As one player is saying their count, another player can check it against a number line.

Developing Numeracy
Numbers and the Number System
Year 1
© A & C Black 1999

- **Count the prints in each picture.**
- **Write the number in the box.**

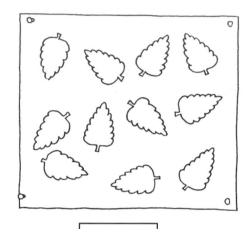
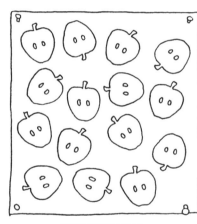

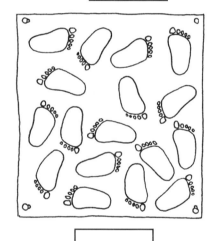

- **Print 12 of your own fingerprints!**

Teachers' note Encourage the children to count by touching the objects in a systematic way, before progressing to counting without touching. Some children may find it helpful to use counters to match the number of prints on each picture. You could also provide a number line to 20 as an additional source of help.

Developing Numeracy
Numbers and the Number System
Year 1
© A & C Black 1999

In the supermarket

- **Count the shopping.**

- **Write the numbers in the boxes.**

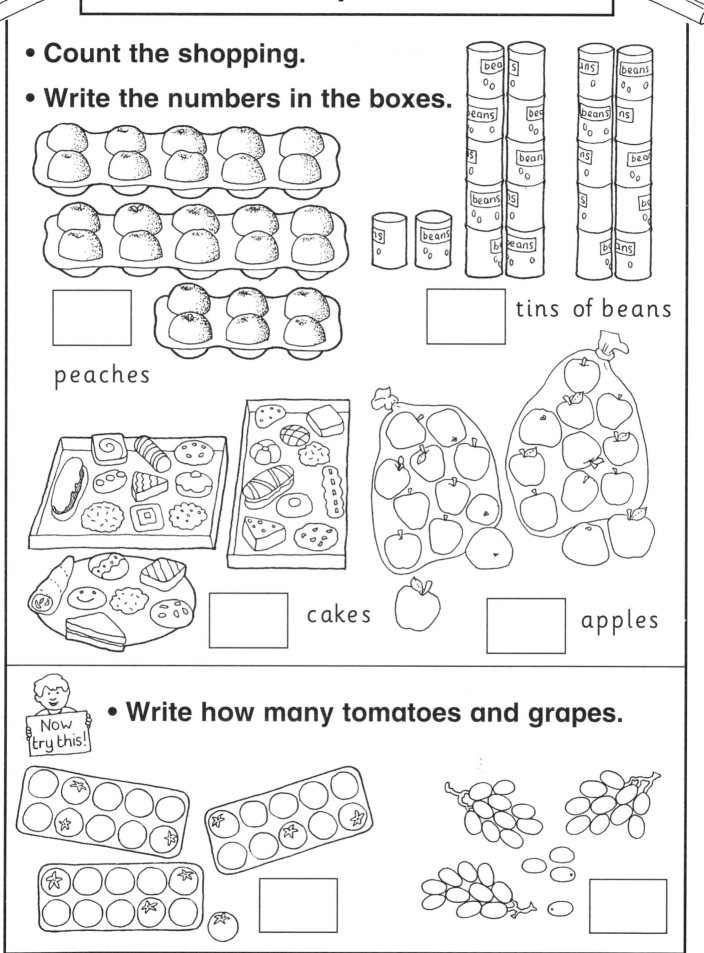

peaches

tins of beans

cakes

apples

- **Write how many tomatoes and grapes.**

Now try this!

Teachers' note Encourage children to count in groups of 2, 5 or 10, as an introduction to what is quite an advanced skill. Show the children how to draw tallies to help them keep a count of a group of objects.

Developing Numeracy
Numbers and the Number System
Year 1
© A & C Black 1999

On the beach

- **Write the missing numbers.**

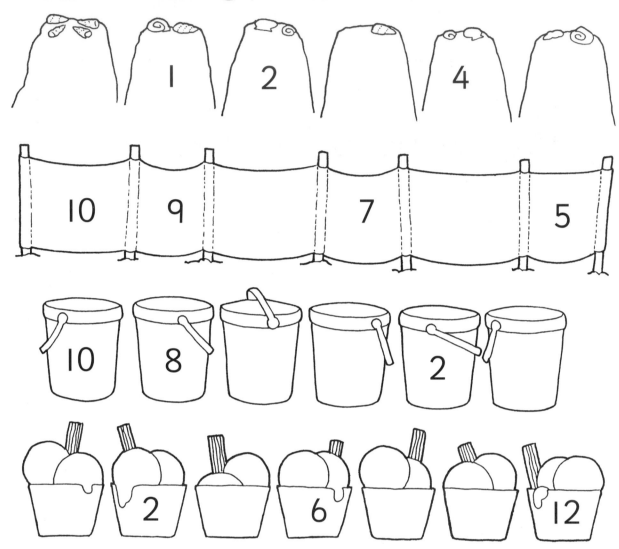

1   2   4

10   9   7   5

10   8   2

2   6   12

Now try this!

- **Write how many**

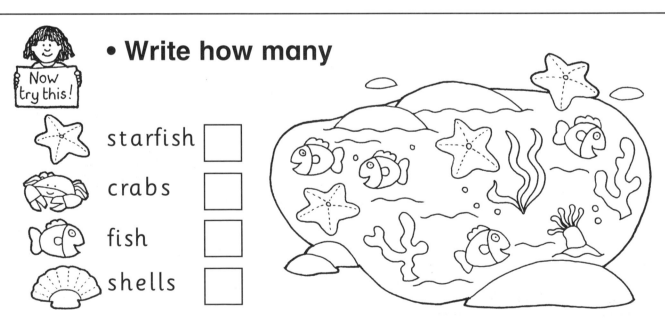

starfish ☐

crabs ☐

fish ☐

shells ☐

Teachers' note Discuss zero with the children, showing it as an empty set and as a position in the counting pattern on a number line or track. It may also be appropriate to show them its use as a place holder in numbers such as 30 and 40. In the extension activity, children may need some help to realise that there are no crabs or shells so the answer is 0.

Developing Numeracy
Numbers and the Number System
Year 1
© **A & C Black 1999**

- **Write the missing numbers.**

50   40   30

0   5   10

0   10   20

- **Write how many**

cones	
signs	
bridges	
bicycles	
people	

Teachers' note You could provide a 100-square as reference for children who need additional help with this activity.

Developing Numeracy
Numbers and the Number System
Year 1
© A & C Black 1999

- **Write the missing numbers on the roller coaster.**

- **Fill in the missing numbers.**

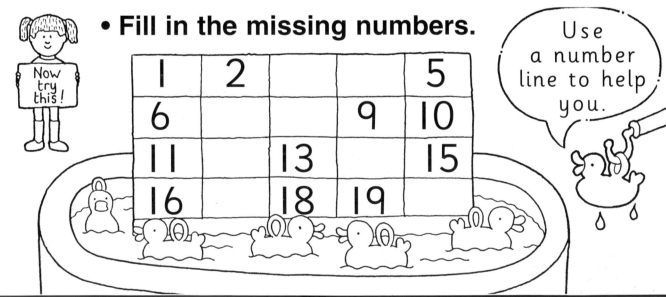

1	2			5
6			9	10
11		13		15
16		18	19	

Use a number line to help you.

Teachers' note You could provide a number line or track as reference for children who need additional help with this activity.

Developing Numeracy
Numbers and the Number System
Year 1
© A & C Black 1999

Do it yourself!

- **Write the missing numbers on this 100-square.**

Use a 100-square to help you.

1	2		4		6	7		9	
11	12		14		16	17		19	
21	22		24		26	27		29	
31	32		34		36	37		39	
41	42		44		46	47		49	
51	52		54		56	57		59	
61	62		64		66	67		69	
71	72		74		76	77		79	
81	82		84		86	87		89	
91	92		94		96	97		99	

- **Write the missing numbers in the spaces.**

 Now try this!

 10   40   50

 80   70   30

   55   65

- **Cover 2 numbers. Ask a friend to say what the hidden numbers are.**

Teachers' note To introduce the activity, talk about the patterns involved with counting in tens and model the process from a variety of starting numbers. Provide each child with a complete 100-square (page 61) to use as reference during the activity. Provide counters for the children to use for the extension activity.

**Developing Numeracy
Numbers and the Number System
Year 1**
© A & C Black 1999

Jumping in 2s

David jumps in 2s!

• **Continue the lines to show where he lands.**

| 0 | 1 | 2 | 3 | 4 | 5 | 6 | 7 | 8 | 9 | 10 | 11 |

| 1 | 2 | 3 | 4 | 5 | 6 | 7 | 8 | 9 | 10 | 11 | 12 |

| 10 | 11 | 12 | 13 | 14 | 15 | 16 | 17 | 18 | 19 | 20 |

| 7 | 8 | 9 | 10 | 11 | 12 | 13 | 14 | 15 | 16 |

| 6 | 7 | 8 | 9 | 10 | 11 | 12 | 13 | 14 | 15 |

Now try this!

• **Count in 2s to find the paths across.**

start Colour the path blue.

start Colour the path red.

2   4   10   12   14   18   **home**   20

6   9   16   17   **home**   19

1   8   11

3   5   7   13   15

Teachers' note Link this activity with the idea of odd and even numbers, both of which involve counting in twos, one starting at zero and the other at one.

Developing Numeracy
Numbers and the Number System
Year 1
© A & C Black 1999

Even numbers

- **Colour** $\boxed{2}$, $\boxed{4}$ **and** $\boxed{6}$ **yellow.**

All the numbers you colour are even numbers.

- **Continue the pattern, counting in 2s.**

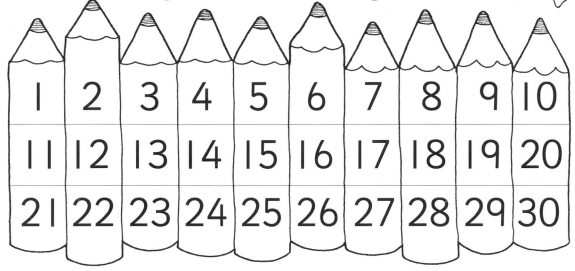

1	2	3	4	5	6	7	8	9	10
11	12	13	14	15	16	17	18	19	20
21	22	23	24	25	26	27	28	29	30

- **Complete these even number patterns.**

2 4 6 __ __ __ __ __ __

20 18 16 __ __ __ __ __ __

Now try this!

- **Colour the crayons with even numbers.**

Even numbers end with 0, 2, 4, 6 or 8.

4   13   11

17   1   2   25

3

19   18   6   9   14

20

10   8   15   12   5   16   7

Teachers' note Discuss the colour pattern in the first activity before going on to the remaining activities. Ask the children if they can see the pattern of the 'units' digits for each even number.

Developing Numeracy
Numbers and the Number System
Year 1
© A & C Black 1999

- **Count in 2s.**

- **Write the number of animals in each group.**

 • How many legs in each group?

Count in 2s.

Teachers' note To introduce the activity, count orally as a class from 1 to 20, whispering the odd numbers and shouting the even numbers to emphasise the pattern of twos.

Developing Numeracy
Numbers and the Number System
Year 1
© A & C Black 1999

Odd numbers

- **Colour** $\boxed{1}$, $\boxed{3}$ **and** $\boxed{5}$ **green.**
- **Continue the pattern, counting in 2s.**

All the numbers you colour are odd numbers.

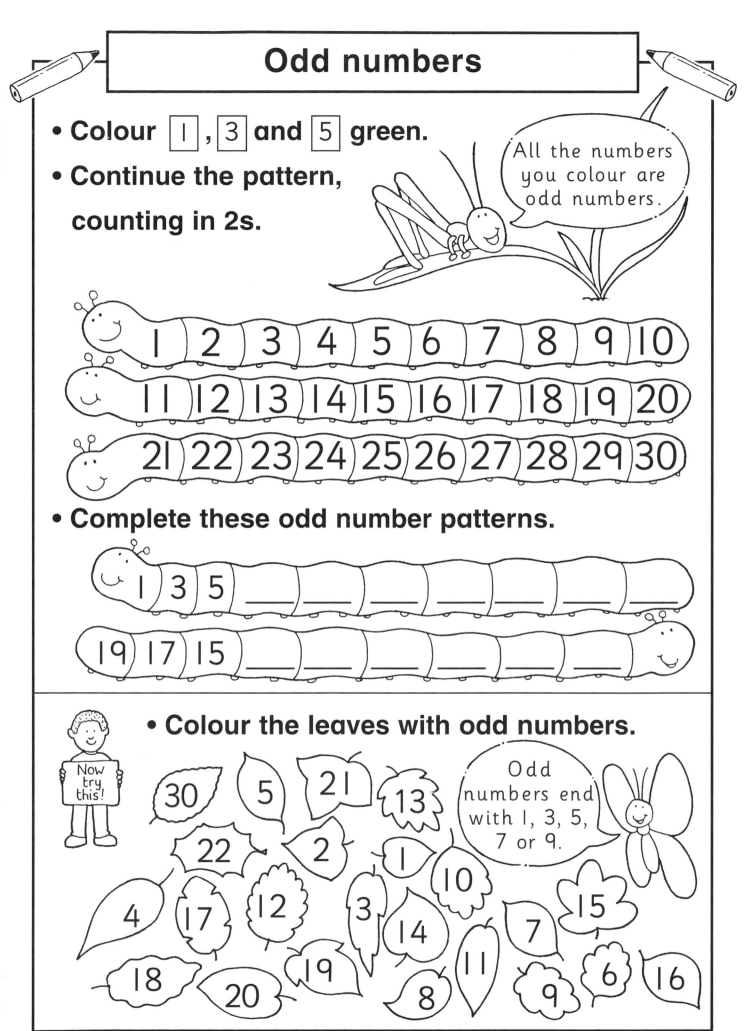

1	2	3	4	5	6	7	8	9	10
11	12	13	14	15	16	17	18	19	20
21	22	23	24	25	26	27	28	29	30

- **Complete these odd number patterns.**

1 3 5 ___ ___ ___ ___ ___ ___ ___

19 17 15 ___ ___ ___ ___ ___ ___ ___

Now try this!

- **Colour the leaves with odd numbers.**

Odd numbers end with 1, 3, 5, 7 or 9.

30 5 21 13
22 2 1
4 17 12 3 10 15
18 14 7
20 19 8 11 9 6 16

Teachers' note Discuss the colour pattern in the first activity before going on to the remaining activities. Ask the children if they can see the pattern of the 'units' digits for each odd number.

Developing Numeracy
Numbers and the Number System
Year 1
© A & C Black 1999

Odds and evens

• **Cut out these cards.**

Teachers' note Photocopy this sheet on to A3 card. In pairs, the children could play 'odd and even numbers snap' using a set of cards that can include numbers alone or both the numbers and word cards. To win, a player must spot matching even or odd cards, for example, '2 and 4' or '1 and odd'. Alternatively, a pair of children could use a shuffled set of number cards and turn over one card at a time. The winner is the one who is the faster to say whether the number is odd or even.

Developing Numeracy
Numbers and the Number System
Year 1
© A & C Black 1999

This frog jumps in 5s!

- **Continue the line to show where the frog lands.**

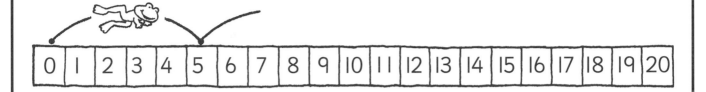

0 | 1 | 2 | 3 | 4 | 5 | 6 | 7 | 8 | 9 | 10 | 11 | 12 | 13 | 14 | 15 | 16 | 17 | 18 | 19 | 20

- **Write the missing numbers on the lilypads.**

  Count in 5s.

5 10 15 __ __ __ __ __ __

30 25 20 __ __ __ __

__ __ 10 __ __ 25 __ 40

- **Draw a line from each frog to the lilypad where it should be sitting.**

Teachers' note Ask children to hold up five fingers every time they add five in a count. A group of children could do this sitting in a circle, so that everyone's hands can be seen and the total number of fingers counted.

Developing Numeracy
Numbers and the Number System
Year 1
© A & C Black 1999

23

Jump, rabbit, jump!

This rabbit jumps in 3s!

- Continue the line to show where the rabbit lands.

| 0 | 1 | 2 | 3 | 4 | 5 | 6 | 7 | 8 | 9 | 10 | 11 | 12 | 13 | 14 | 15 | 16 | 17 | 18 | 19 | 20 | 21 | 22 | 23 | 24 | 25 | 26 | 27 | 28 |

- Join the dots counting in 3s.

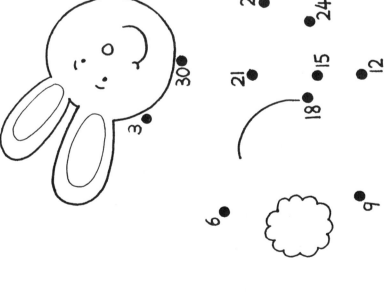

- Write the missing numbers in the carrots. Count in 3s.

Now try this!

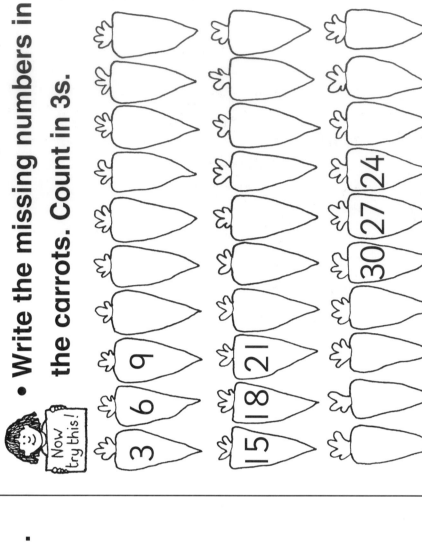

Developing Numeracy
Numbers and the Number System Year 1

Teachers' note To introduce this challenging activity, provide each child with a number line and practise counting in threes, whispering 1 and 2, and shouting 3 (1, 2, **3**, 4, 5, **6**, 7, 8, **9**) and so on.

- **Write the missing numbers in the spaces.**

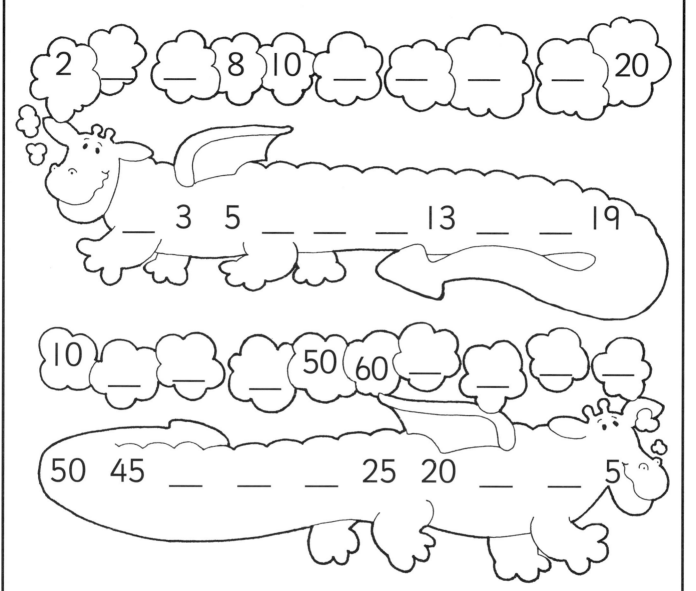

2 __ __ 8 10 __ __ __ __ 20

__ 3 5 __ __ __ 13 __ __ 19

10 __ __ __ __ 50 60 __ __ __ __

50 45 __ __ __ 25 20 __ __ 5

 **Now try this!**

- **See how far you can count out loud.**

Count in 3s starting with **3**.	Count in 10s starting with **10**.
Count in 2s starting with **2**.	Count in 5s starting with **5**.

Teachers' note For the extension activity put the children in pairs, one saying the count, the other checking with a 100-square (page 61).

**Developing Numeracy
Numbers and the Number System
Year 1**
© A & C Black 1999

Sock patterns

• **Write the missing numbers on each sock.**

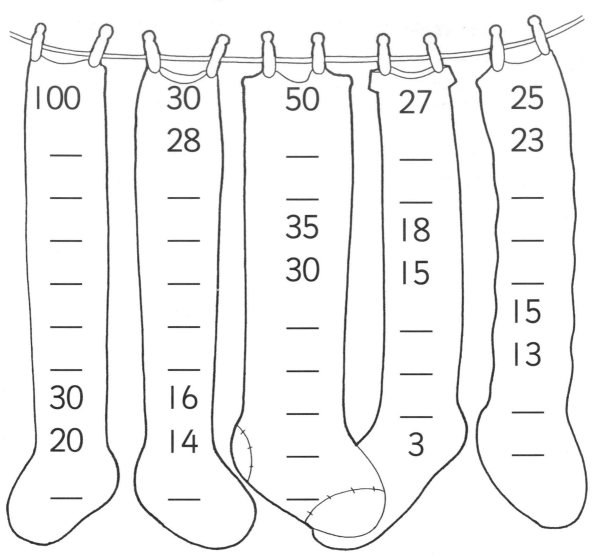

Sock 1	Sock 2	Sock 3	Sock 4	Sock 5
100	30	50	27	25
—	28	—	—	23
—	—	—	18	—
—	—	35	15	—
—	—	30	—	15
30	16	—	—	13
20	14	—	3	—
—	—	—		—

Now try this!

• **Work with a friend.**

• **Take turns to count.**

> Use a 100-square to check your counting.

Start with **100**. Count back in 10s.

Start with **100**. Count back in 5s.

Start with **20**. Count back in 2s.

Start with **3**. Count in odd numbers.

Teachers' note For the extension activity put the children in pairs, one saying the count, the other checking with a 100-square (page 61).

Developing Numeracy
Numbers and the Number System
Year 1
© A & C Black 1999

Hopping spider game

- **Take turns to roll the dice and move your counter.**

- **Your turn ends when you land on a spider.**

When you roll	•	move in 1s.
When you roll	••	move in 2s.
When you roll	••	go to 28. Count back in 2s.
When you roll	::	move in 10s.
When you roll	::.	move in 5s.
When you roll	:::	go to 25. Count back in 5s.

start →

Teachers' note Children should practise counting on or back on a number line before playing this game. To win, a child must land exactly on the number 30. This page could be copied onto A3 sheets.

Developing Numeracy
Numbers and the Number System
Year 1
© A & C Black 1999

- **Trace over the number.**
- **Write the number, starting on the dot.**

1   1   1   1   1   1

2   2   2   2   2   2

3   3   3   3   3   3

4   4   4   4   4   4

5   5   5   5   5   5

- **Count the sweets.**
- **Write the number in the box.**

Teachers' note Left-handed children may form numerals in a different way, particularly the numeral 5. See **Year R** for activities to introduce children to writing numbers.

**Developing Numeracy
Numbers and the Number System
Year 1**
© A & C Black 1999

- **Trace over the number.**
- **Write the number, starting on the dot.**

6

7

8

9

10

- **Count the mice.**
- **Write the number in the box.**

Teachers' note Left-handed children may form numerals in a different way, particularly the numeral 8. See **Year R** for activities to introduce children to writing numbers.

Developing Numeracy
Numbers and the Number System
Year 1
© A & C Black 1999

Birds' nests

- Trace over each number.
- Draw lines to match the numbers and the nests.

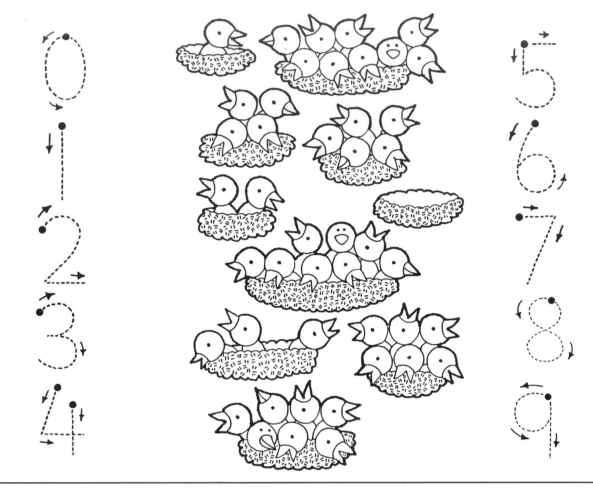

 • Write the number in each box.

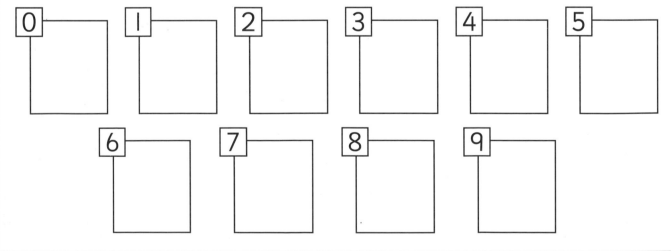

Developing Numeracy
Numbers and the Number System
Year 1
© A & C Black 1999

Five fat sausages

• **Draw lines to match the numbers to the words.**

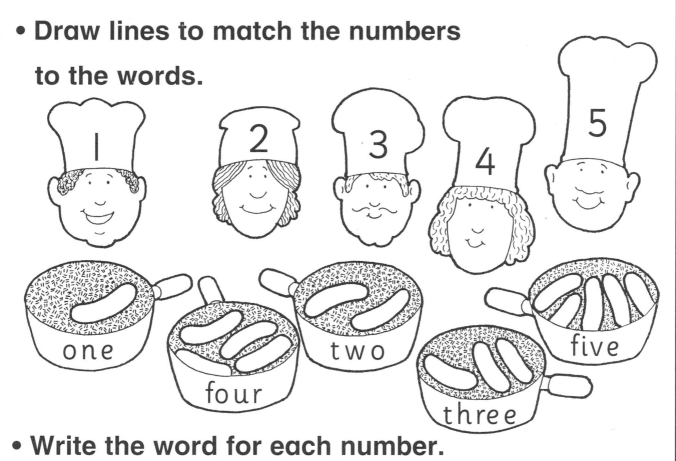

• **Write the word for each number.**

| 1 | o | n | e |

| 2 | _ | _ | _ |

| 3 | _ | _ | _ | _ |

| 4 | _ | _ | _ |

| 5 | _ | _ | _ |

Now try this!

• **Count the eggs on each plate.**

• **Write the number word in the box.**

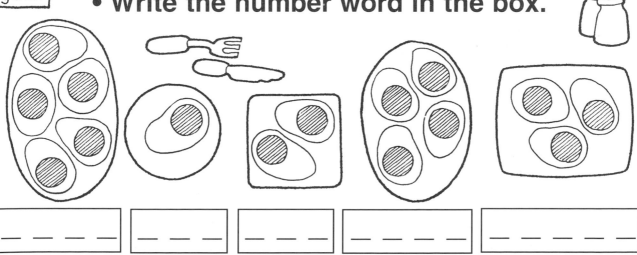

Teachers' note To introduce this activity, say the rhyme 'Five fat sausages' with the class before using the sheet.

Developing Numeracy
Numbers and the Number System
Year 1
© A & C Black 1999

Balloon numbers

- **Copy the number words in the balloons.**
- **Match each balloon to a clown.**

six

eight

ten
_ _ _ _

_ _ _ _ _

seven
_ _ _ _ _

nine
_ _ _ _

9   7   10   6   8

- **Count the balloons.**
- **Write the number word for each bunch.**

Now try this!

_ _ _ _ _	_ _ _ _	_ _ _ _	_ _ _ _ _	_ _ _ _

Developing Numeracy
Numbers and the Number System
Year 1
© A & C Black 1999

On the buses

- **Trace over all the numbers.**
- **Write the number words.**
- **Match the numbers to the buses.**

11   11   11

12   12   12

13   13   13

14   14   14

15   15   15

twelve _____

fourteen _____

eleven _____

fifteen _____

thirteen _____

- **Write the number on each bus.**

Now try this!

fifteen   twelve   eleven   thirteen

Developing Numeracy
Numbers and the Number System
Year 1
© A & C Black 1999

Sweets

- **Trace over each number.**
- **Count the sweets in the jars.**
- **Match the numbers to the jars.**

16   16   16

17   17   17

18   18   18

19   19   19

20   20   20

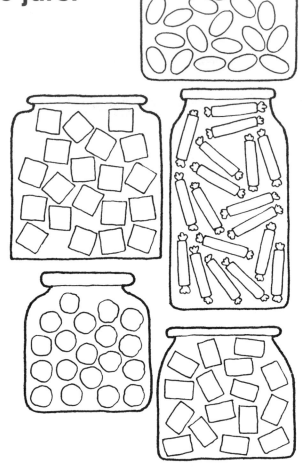

- **Write the number word on each sweet.**

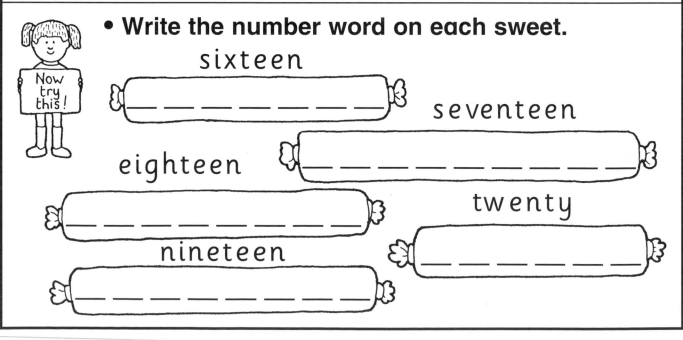

sixteen

seventeen

eighteen

twenty

nineteen

Now try this!

Developing Numeracy
Numbers and the Number System
Year 1
© A & C Black 1999

The maths menace

- **The maths menace has stolen some numbers from the grid.**

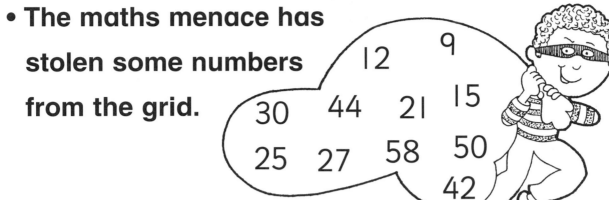

12   9
30   44   21   15
25   27   58   50
42

- **Write the numbers on the grid.**

1	2	3				7			10
11		13				17			20
		24							
						37	38		
				45	46				
	52				56				60

- **Fill in all the other missing numbers.**

- **Write the missing numbers in the boxes.**

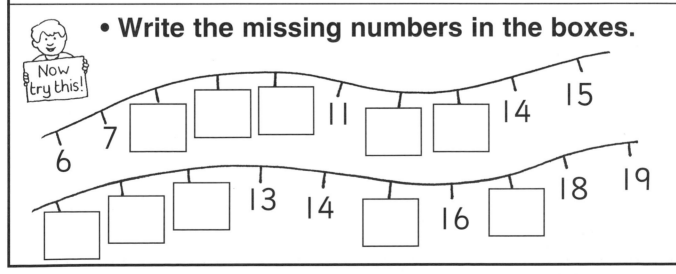

6 7 [ ] [ ] [ ] 11 [ ] [ ] 14 15

[ ] [ ] 13 14 [ ] 16 [ ] 18 19

Now try this!

Teachers' note Children can use a 100-square (page 61) to help them with this activity.

Developing Numeracy
Numbers and the Number System
Year 1
© A & C Black 1999

In the garden

• **Join each butterfly to the correct flower.**

Some of the numbers are teen numbers.

• **Write the missing numbers in the boxes.**

Now try this!

Teachers' note Make sure children understand the term 'teen' number. You could use the arrow cards (page 62) to show how, for example, 10 and 6 makes 16.

Developing Numeracy
Numbers and the Number System
Year 1
© A & C Black 1999

36

Numbers on an abacus

- **What number is shown on each abacus?**

- **Write the number in the box.**

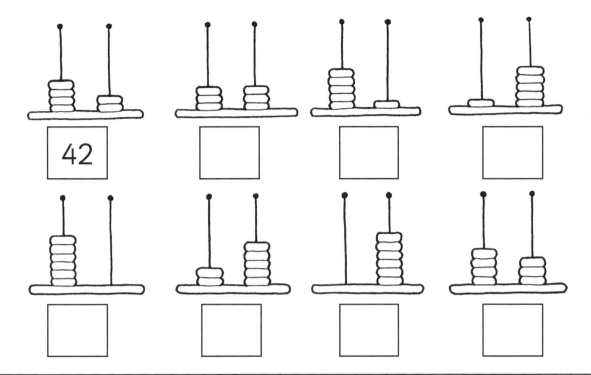

42

- **Draw beads on each abacus to match the numbers in the boxes.**

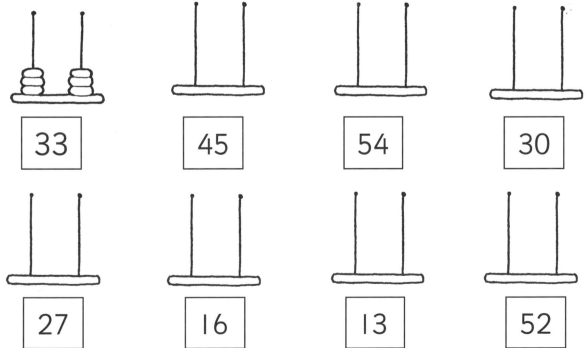

33

45

54

30

27

16

13

52

Teachers' note Ask children to use an abacus to show the different numbers they can make with eight beads.

Developing Numeracy
Numbers and the Number System
Year 1
© A & C Black 1999

Signposts

- **Write the number for each signpost.**

1 0	2 0	1 0	2 0
6	1	4	2
16	☐	☐	☐

3 0	3 0	4 0	4 0
5	3	3	9
☐	☐	☐	☐

- **Now write signpost numbers for these.**

Now try this!

| 28 | 47 | 11 | 32 |

Teachers' note Use the arrow cards (page 62) to show expanded notation (for example, 20 + 4 = 24) as an introduction to this activity.

Developing Numeracy
Numbers and the Number System
Year 1
© A & C Black 1999

Building bricks

• **Write the missing numbers in the boxes.**

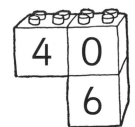

$40 + 6 = 46$

$\boxed{} + 5 = 15$

$60 + 8 = \boxed{}$

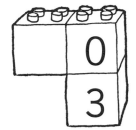

$30 + 3 = 33$

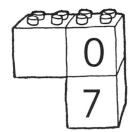

$90 + 2 = 92$

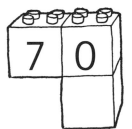

$70 + 1 = 71$

$20 + 9 = \boxed{}$

$50 + 7 = \boxed{}$

$80 + 4 = \boxed{}$

• **Write the missing numbers in the bricks.**

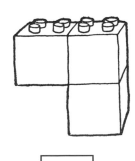

18

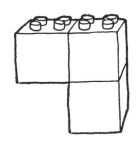

43

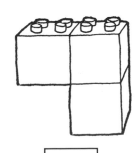

36

Teachers' note Use the arrow cards (page 62) to show expanded notation (for example, 20 + 4 = 24) as an introduction to this activity.

Developing Numeracy
Numbers and the Number System
Year 1
© A & C Black 1999

Train carriages

- **Colour blue the number that is** less.

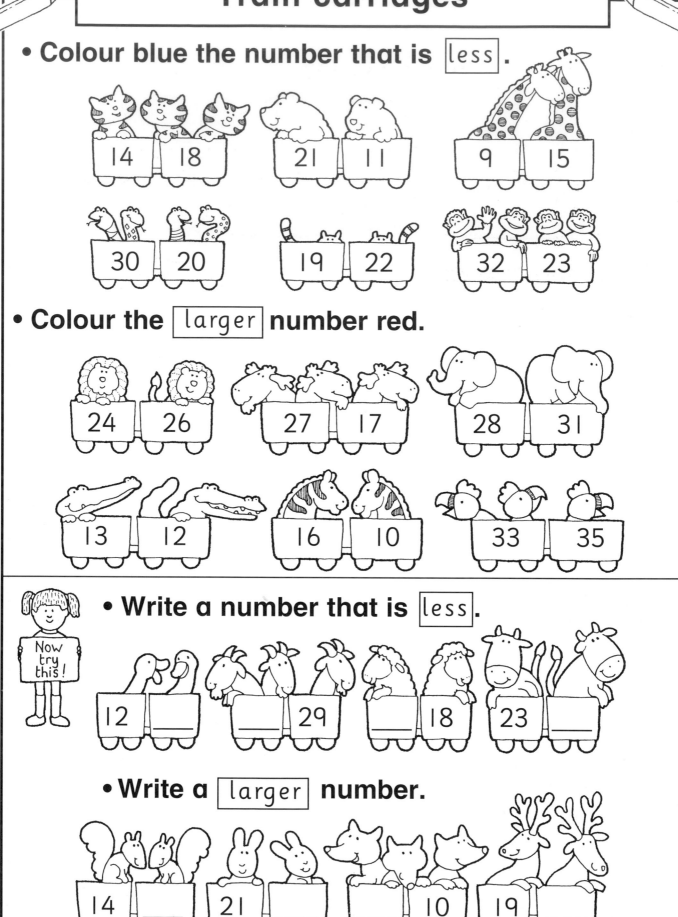

14	18
21	11
9	15
30	20
19	22
32	23

- **Colour the** larger **number red.**

24	26
27	17
28	31
13	12
16	10
33	35

- **Write a number that is** less.

12		29		18	23	

- **Write a** larger **number.**

14		21		10	19

Teachers' note Provide a number track or 100-square (page 61) to help the children to compare two numbers. Revise vocabulary such as 'less', 'fewer', 'smaller', 'larger'. In the extension activity, encourage the children to write a different number on each carriage.

Developing Numeracy
Numbers and the Number System
Year 1
© A & C Black 1999

I more

• Write I [m o r e] in each cloud.

16 17
19
13
21
27
10

• Write the new price.

7p   Ip more   p

12p   Ip more   p

15p   Ip more   p

28p   Ip more   p

• Join each cloud to a raindrop that is I [m o r e].

Now try this!

23   12   29
17   9   20   11
10   30   18   12   24   21   13

Teachers' note Use a number track to show the children how to find 'one more'. A group of children could stand at the front of the class, holding number cards in order as a human number line. Other children could be invited to come to the front and point out, for example, which number is one more than 11.

Developing Numeracy
Numbers and the Number System
Year 1
© A & C Black 1999

41

I less

• Write I $\boxed{\text{less}}$ in each skittle.

14 13   11   17   9

22   25   20   18

• Write the new price.

10p → 1p less → p   13p → 1p less → p   21p → 1p less → p

29p → 1p less → p   16p → 1p less → p   27p → 1p less → p

• Join each skittle to a number on a bowling ball that is I $\boxed{\text{less}}$.

Now try this!

12   15   24   20

14   11   19   23

Teachers' note Use a number track to show the children how to find 'one less'. A group of children could stand at the front of the class, holding number cards in order as a human number line. Other children could be invited to come to the front and point out, for example, which number is one less than 12.

Developing Numeracy
Numbers and the Number System
Year 1
© A & C Black 1999

42

10 less

- **What is 10 `less` than each of these numbers?**
- **Write your answers in the boxes.**

27 □ 19 □ 67 □ 34 □ 96 □

80 □ 22 □ 75 □ 59 □ 100 □

- **Write the missing numbers.**

Now try this!

60
50

95
75
55
20

41
31

Teachers' note You could provide a 100-square (page 61) to help the children with this activity.

**Developing Numeracy
Numbers and the Number System**
Year 1
© A & C Black 1999

43

• **Follow the paths. Write 10** more **in each space.**

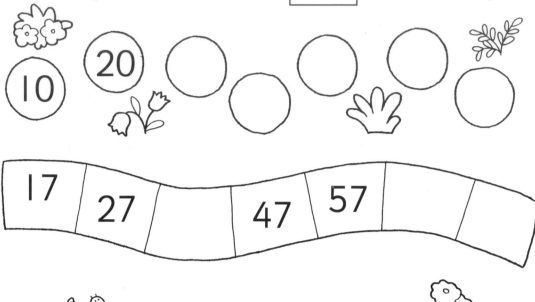

⑩ ⑳ ◯ ◯ ◯ ◯

| 17 | 27 | | | 47 | 57 | | |

| 2 | 12 | | 32 | 42 | | | 72 | 82 |

• **Write the new price on each label.**

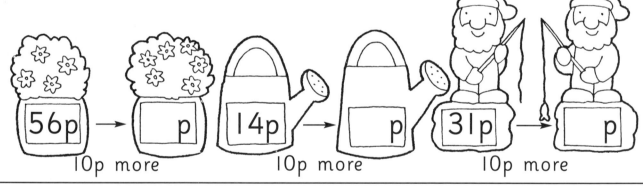

| 56p | → | p | 14p | → | p | 31p | → | p |

10p more   10p more   10p more

• **Find two paths across the garden.**
• **Colour the squares, counting in tens.**

start → 8 18 17 82 56 61 71 84 95
         7 28 38 48 51 63 74 81 98 ← home
         4 14 31 41 58 68 78 88 91 ← home
start → 11 21 23 14 85 60 70 80 92

Teachers' note You could provide a 100-square (page 61) to help the children with this activity. Suggest that children attempting the extension activity colour the two paths with two different colours.

Developing Numeracy
Numbers and the Number System
Year 1
© A & C Black 1999

44

Sale!

- **Write the new price for each toy.**

28p

1p off

now ☐ p

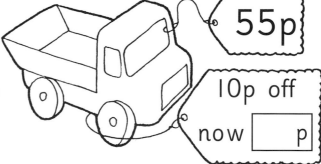

55p

10p off

now ☐ p

99p

10p off

now ☐ p

37p

1p off

now ☐ p

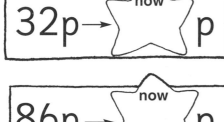
Now try this!

- **Write 1p** more .

32p → now ☐ p

86p → now ☐ p

7p → now ☐ p

- **Write 10p** more .

43p → now ☐ p

68p → now ☐ p

70p → now ☐ p

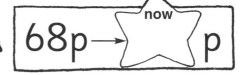

**Developing Numeracy
Numbers and the Number System
Year 1
© A & C Black 1999**

45

More and less

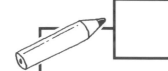

- **Look at the number line.**

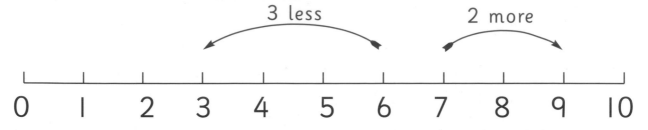

3 less   2 more

0 1 2 3 4 5 6 7 8 9 10

- **Write 3 less .**

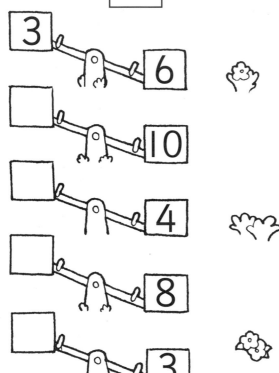

3	6
	10
	4
	8
	3

- **Write 2 more .**

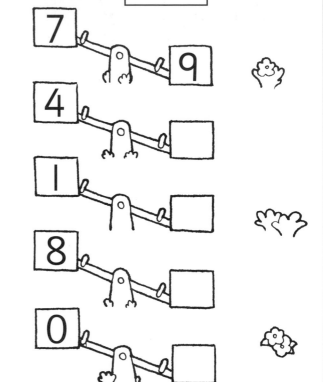

7	9
4	
1	
8	
0	

- **Draw an arrow on each number line to show:**

Now try this!

4 more than 9

7 8 9 10 11 12 13 14 15

5 less than 12

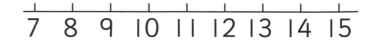

7 8 9 10 11 12 13 14 15

2 less than 15

7 8 9 10 11 12 13 14 15

**Developing Numeracy
Numbers and the Number System
Year 1
© A & C Black 1999**

Missing pieces

- ## Write the missing numbers on each grid.

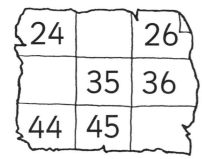

Use a 100-square to help you.

24		26
	35	36
44	45	

61	62			65
	72	73		
81		83	84	85

	77	78		80
86	87			90
96		98	99	

11		13	
21		23	24
	32		34

4		6	7		
	15	16		18	19
24	25		27	28	

	34		36
43		45	
	54		56

Now try this!

- ## Write the missing numbers.

35			38	
45		47	48	49
		57		

	68	69		
77			79	80
85		87	88	
95				

Teachers' note This is a particularly challenging activity, and each child will need a 100-square (page 61) to use as reference.

Developing Numeracy
Numbers and the Number System
Year 1
© A & C Black 1999

Ladybirds

- Count the spots on each ladybird.
- Join the ladybirds on each leaf in order.

  Start with the most spots.

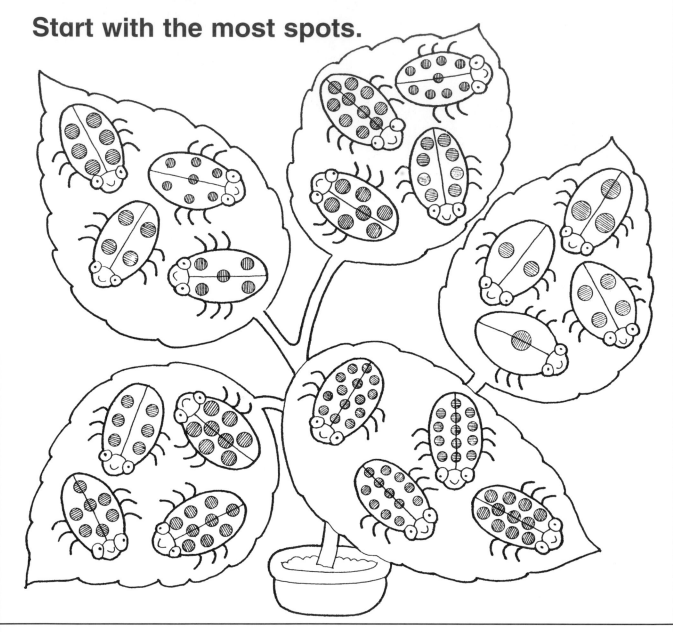

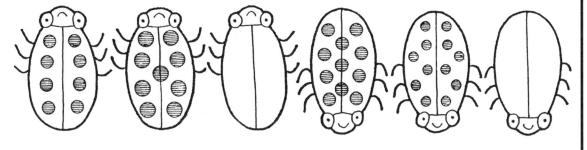

- Draw spots to continue the pattern.

Now try this!

Developing Numeracy
Numbers and the Number System
Year 1
© A & C Black 1999

Washing day

- ## Colour yellow the largest number on each line.

13 19 15 17   21 11 31 12

18 14 10 8   22 25 28 23

- ## Colour green the smallest number on each line.

19 21 12 8   18 17 23 22

32 29 28 30   30 10 20 22

- ## Write the numbers in order on the shirts.
- ## Start with the smallest number.

Now try this!

16   18   14   21   23   19   20

Teachers' note Ask groups of children to make any two-digit numbers with their arrow cards and then arrange themselves in a row to show the order of the numbers they have made. Point out to the children that they can put numbers in order even if some are missing from a sequence.

Developing Numeracy
Numbers and the Number System
Year 1
© A & C Black 1999

School fair

• **Write the missing number in each space.**

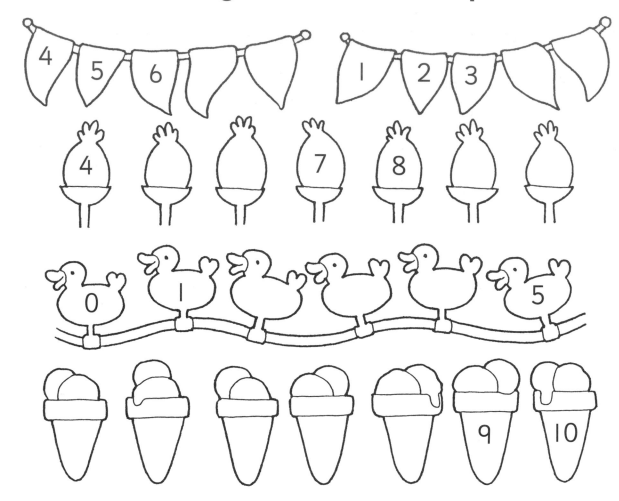

• **Write the numbers in order on the bottles.**

• **Start with the smallest number.**

Teachers' note As an introduction to the activity, give a different number card to each child in a group and ask them to stand in order. Ask questions about order and comparison, for example, Which is bigger, seven or nine? What number comes between six and eight?

Developing Numeracy
Numbers and the Number System
Year 1
© A & C Black 1999

50

Number trees

- **Write the numbers in order.**
- **Start with the largest number.**

Teachers' note For the extension activity, make sure the children realise that there are two separate dot-to-dot puzzles and that some numbers are missing from the sequences.

Developing Numeracy
Numbers and the Number System
Year 1
© A & C Black 1999

51

Shoe shop

• **Write the next number on each shoe.**

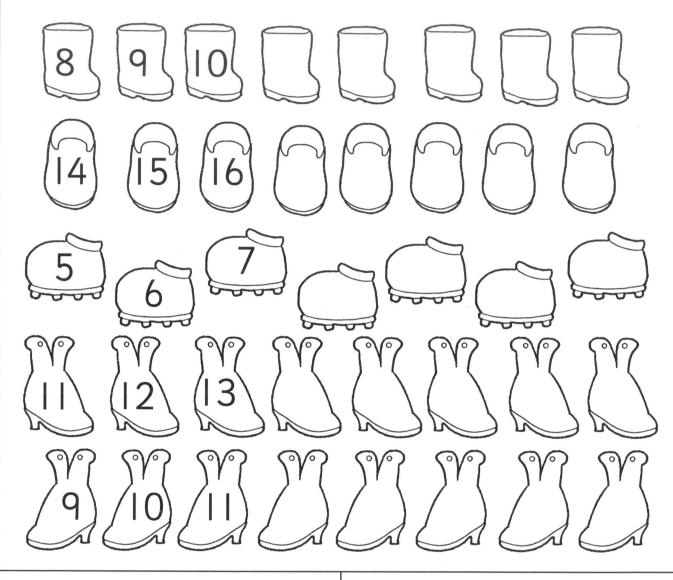

• **Join the dots.**

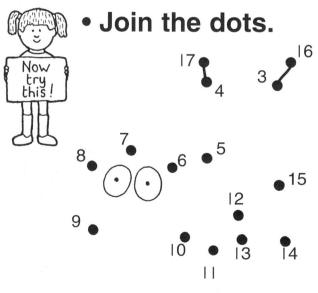

Start with the smallest number!

52

Developing Numeracy
Numbers and the Number System
Year 1
© A & C Black 1999

Fun in the sand

• **Write each group of numbers in order.**

Start with the smallest number.

19   8
  15
20   11

8 11 ___ ___ ___ ___

9   17
  7
12   14

___ ___ ___ ___ ___

16   18
  6
3   13

___ ___ ___ ___ ___

20   10
  5
7   17

___ ___ ___ ___ ___

• **Write the numbers in order.**

Now try this!

Start with the largest number.

20 19

18   20   11   8   2   15   13   19

Developing Numeracy
Numbers and the Number System
Year 1
© A & C Black 1999

53

Crocodile numbers

• **Write the missing numbers on the crocodiles.**

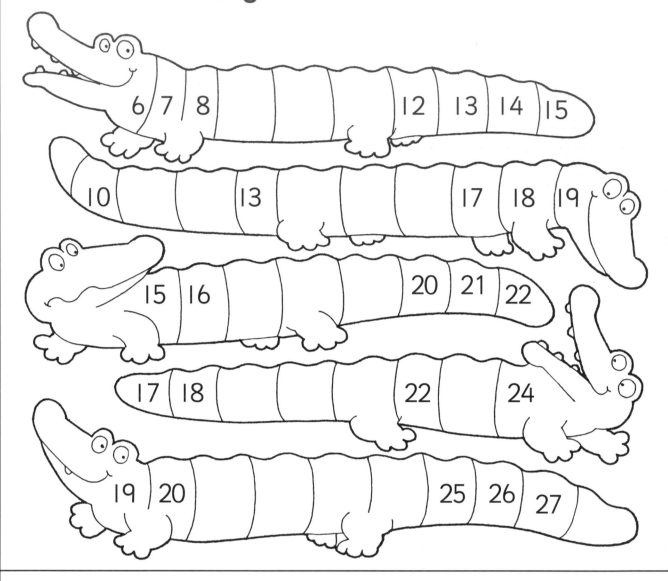

• **Write the numbers in order on each canoe.**
• **Start with the smallest number.**

12 16 17 14 13 15   22 20 18 23 19 21

Teachers' note Point out to the children that they can put numbers in order even if some are missing from a sequence.

Developing Numeracy
Numbers and the Number System
Year 1
© A & C Black 1999

Most and least

- ## Draw a circle round the purse with $\boxed{\text{most}}$ money.

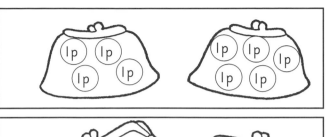
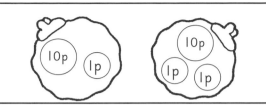
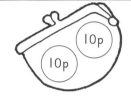

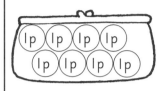
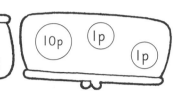

- ## Draw a circle round the purse with $\boxed{\text{least}}$ money.

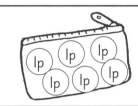

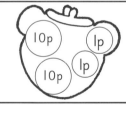
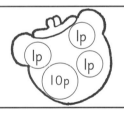
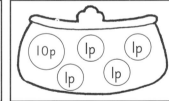
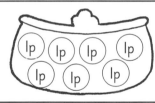

- ## Draw coins to total $\boxed{\text{more}}$ than 11p.

- ## Draw coins to total $\boxed{\text{less}}$ than 20p.

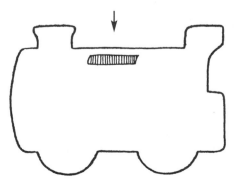

Teachers' note For the extension activity limit the children to using 1p and 10p coins only. They can then go on to explore the use of other coins as a separate activity, keeping a record of the combinations of coins they use. The children could be given toy money to work with.

Developing Numeracy
Numbers and the Number System
Year 1
© A & C Black 1999

The bookshop

- **Write the prices in order.**

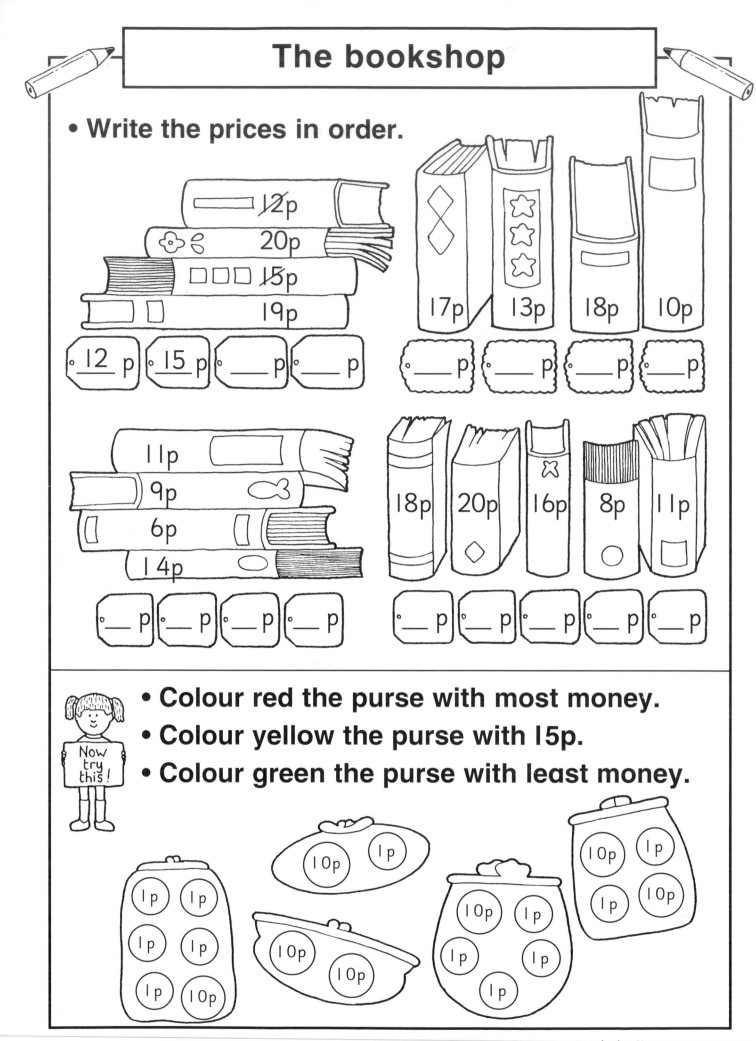

Book stack prices: 12p, 20p, 15p, 19p

Tags: |12 p | |15 p | ___ p | ___ p |

Standing books: 17p, 13p, 18p, 10p

Tags: ___ p | ___ p | ___ p | ___ p

Book stack prices: 11p, 9p, 6p, 14p

Tags: ___ p | ___ p | ___ p | ___ p

Standing books: 18p, 20p, 16p, 8p, 11p

Tags: ___ p | ___ p | ___ p | ___ p | ___ p

- **Colour red the purse with most money.**
- **Colour yellow the purse with 15p.**
- **Colour green the purse with least money.**

Now try this!

Purses: 1p 1p 1p 1p 1p 10p | 10p 1p | 10p 10p | 10p 1p 1p 1p 1p | 10p 1p 1p 10p

Developing Numeracy
Numbers and the Number System
Year 1
© A & C Black 1999

Swimming gala

- **Draw a line from each swimmer to the correct box.**

finish

| 1st | 2nd | 3rd | 4th | 5th |

- **Fill in the missing positions.**

| | | 3rd | | | 6th | | | | 10th |

- **Cut out the cards and put them in order.**

Now try this!

| 2nd | 8th | 12th | 6th | 11th | 3rd |
| 9th | 5th | 1st | 4th | 10th | 7th |

Teachers' note As an addition to the extension activity, the children could set out or draw a row of twelve toy cars as if finishing a race and then match the cards to positions of the cars.

Developing Numeracy
Numbers and the Number System
Year 1
© A & C Black 1999

Guess how many?

- Estimate **how many sheep are in each field.**

estimate ☐   estimate ☐   estimate ☐

- **Now** count **them.**

count ☐   count ☐   count ☐

- **Estimate how many ducklings are on each pond.**

- **Now count them.**

estimate ☐   estimate ☐   estimate ☐

count ☐   count ☐   count ☐

Teachers' note Emphasise to the children that they do not need to count a group of objects to estimate how many there are. You could introduce or reinforce this activity by asking the children to estimate and then count a number of cubes or beads. Ensure that the children are familiar with the language of estimating, using vocabulary such as 'guess', 'roughly' and 'nearly'.

Developing Numeracy
Numbers and the Number System
Year 1
© A & C Black 1999

Classroom estimates

- **Estimate how many in each container.**

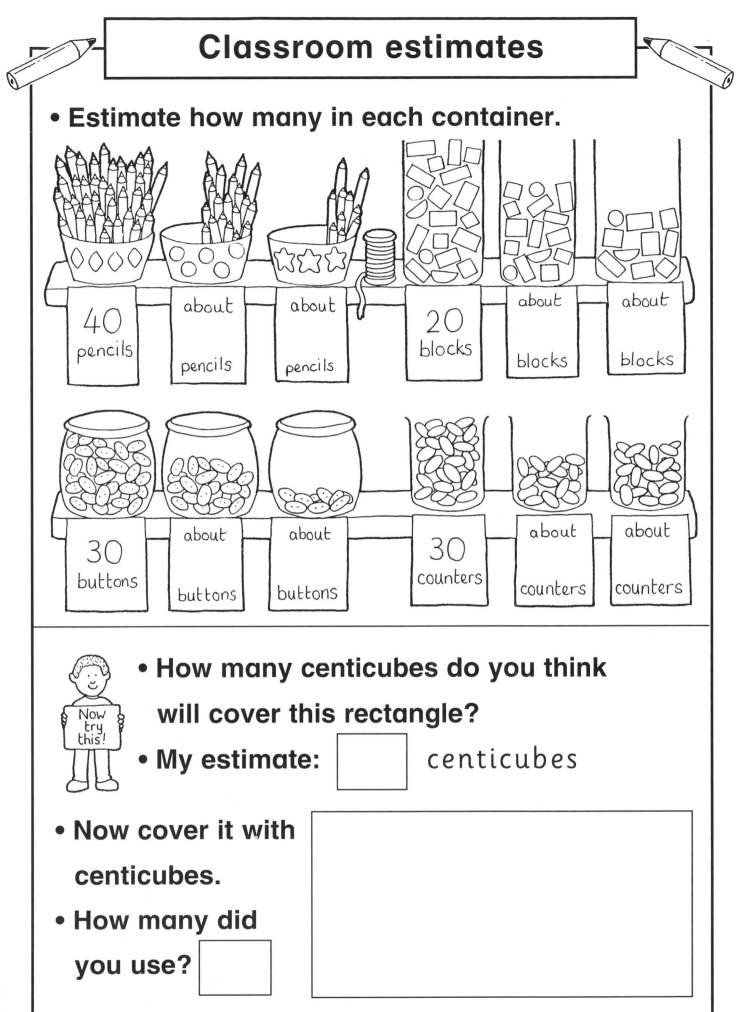

40 pencils

about pencils

about pencils

20 blocks

about blocks

about blocks

30 buttons

about buttons

about buttons

30 counters

about counters

about counters

Now try this!

- **How many centicubes do you think will cover this rectangle?**
- **My estimate:** ☐ centicubes
- **Now cover it with centicubes.**
- **How many did you use?** ☐

Teachers' note Emphasise to the children that they do not need to count a group of objects to estimate how many there are. You could introduce or reinforce this activity by asking the children to estimate and then count a number of cubes or beads. Ensure that the children are familiar with the language of estimating, using vocabulary such as 'guess', 'roughly' and 'nearly'.

Developing Numeracy
Numbers and the Number System
Year 1
© A & C Black 1999

Too many or too few?

- **There are 5 children at the party.**
- **✔ to show if there are too many or too few things on each tray.**

 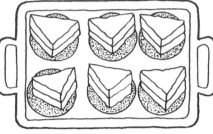 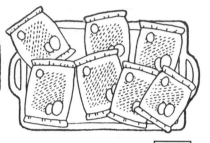

too many ☐   too many ☐   too many ☐

too few ✔   too few ☐   too few ☐

too many ☐ too few ☐   too many ☐ too few ☐

- **Each child needs a balloon and a party hat.**
- **Colour the correct number of balloons and hats for these children.**

Teachers' note As an introduction to this activity, children could practise laying a table for three, four or five people.

Developing Numeracy
Numbers and the Number System
Year 1
© A & C Black 1999

100-square

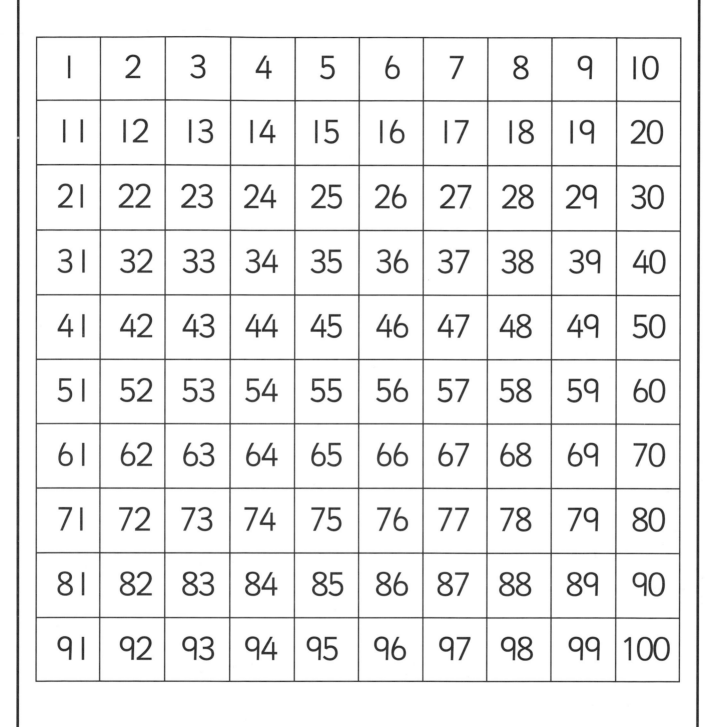

1	2	3	4	5	6	7	8	9	10
11	12	13	14	15	16	17	18	19	20
21	22	23	24	25	26	27	28	29	30
31	32	33	34	35	36	37	38	39	40
41	42	43	44	45	46	47	48	49	50
51	52	53	54	55	56	57	58	59	60
61	62	63	64	65	66	67	68	69	70
71	72	73	74	75	76	77	78	79	80
81	82	83	84	85	86	87	88	89	90
91	92	93	94	95	96	97	98	99	100

Developing Numeracy
Numbers and the Number System
Year 1
© A & C Black 1999

Arrow cards

- Cut out each arrow card.

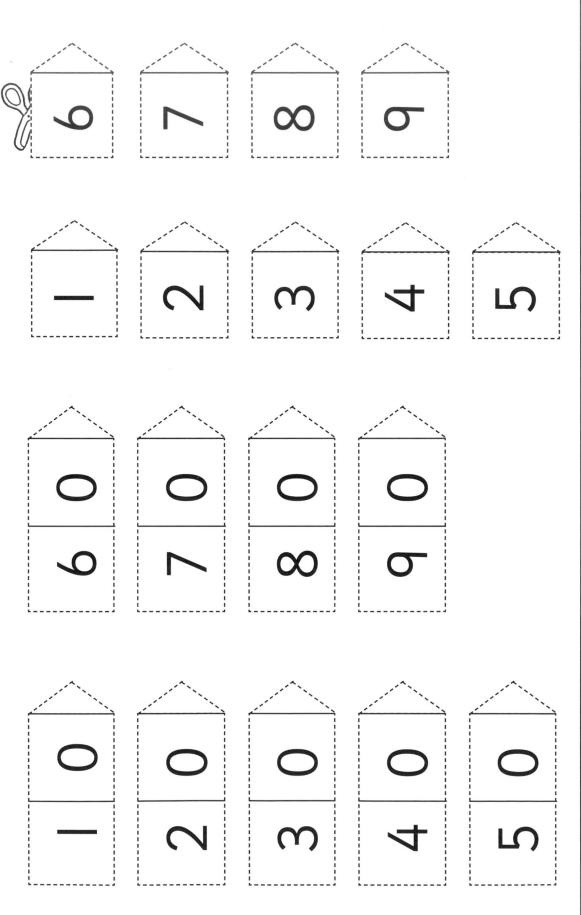

Developing Numeracy
Numbers and the Number System Year 1

Numeral cards 0 to 10

• **Cut out each card.**

0	1	2
3	4	5
6	7	8
9	1	0

Developing Numeracy
Numbers and the Number System
Year 1
© A & C Black 1999

63

Great work

Success

has worked very hard
and can now

Well done!

Developing Numeracy
Numbers and the Number System
Year 1
© A & C Black 1999